Observe

"The quieter you become, the more you can hear.
There is more to life than increasing its speed."

~Mahatma Gandhi

Terrie Mourningdove
Cover Art by Merab Gagiladze

Balboa Press books may be ordered through booksellers or by contacting:

Balboa Press
A Division of Hay House
1663 Liberty Drive
Bloomington, IN 47403
www.balboapress.com
844-682-1282

Because of the dynamic nature of the Internet, any web addresses or links contained in this book may have changed since publication and may no longer be valid. The views expressed in this work are solely those of the author and do not necessarily reflect the views of the publisher, and the publisher hereby disclaims any responsibility for them.

Any people depicted in stock imagery provided by Thinkstock are models, and such images are being used for illustrative purposes only.
Certain stock imagery © Thinkstock.

ISBN: 978-1-5043-7527-6 (sc)
ISBN: 978-1-5043-7528-3 (e)

Library of Congress Control Number: 2017902733

Print information available on the last page.

Balboa Press rev. date: 04/15/2021

BALBOA.PRESS
A DIVISION OF HAY HOUSE

CONTENTS

INTRODUCTION

You will get through it . . . If you can observe it .

As living beings, we all share the ability to feel happiness. We sometimes have difficulty obtaining it but when we do, it is not much of a problem for us to enjoy. At the same time, we all share the ability to feel pain and suffering. These present themselves in various ways but whatever form they take, they are always a challenge for us to deal with.

To better understand *what* we are dealing with, we need to make a distinction between pain and suffering. We cannot avoid the occasions of pain in our lives. Suffering however is a different matter because it is more of a mental process that comes from looking at things in a particular way. This is important to know because it tells us that suffering doesn't automatically need to follow pain and that the way in which we look at it can decidedly determine its effect on us.

To use a minor example, let's say that we are driving down the road on our way to an event and get a flat tire. This will certainly make us late and cause a disruption in our plans. We could cuss and scream and have our blood pressure rise as we blame unseen forces for plotting against us, or we could take a mental step back with a deep breath and say to ourselves, "Stuff Happens" . . . then take the necessary steps to get the tire fixed.

In the first part of this example we are *reacting* to the situation. In the second, we are *observing* it. And there is a noticeable difference that we can feel in our bodies from both responses. *Reacting* causes all of our muscles to tighten which makes us feel tense and angry and unable to think clearly. *Observing* allows us to remain objective which helps us to have a calm and clear mind with which to solve our problem.

If we learn how to observe, it is like giving ourselves a valuable gift that we can carry with us wherever we go. When we remember to use it, we have more control over the way we experience our life rather than being helplessly pulled into the drama of it. Ultimately having this gift prevents us from thinking that we are victims of our world and provides us with the power that we need to become its peaceful co-creators.

* * *

Being a better observer can bring great benefits to our body, mind and spirit and provide us with simple but powerful tools to improve the quality of our life's journey.

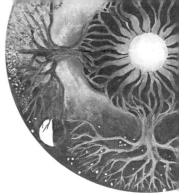

THERE IS MORE THAN MEETS THE EYE

The Inner paints the Outer - The Brush without the Hand –
Its Picture publishes - precise – As in the inner Brand." ~ Emily Dickins

We live in two worlds. One is the outer world of experience and the other is the inner world of thought. And the way in which we experience our world depends entirely on how we think about it.

Our thinking is the result of a process that develops over time. As infants, we didn't do much thinking. We simply lived out of response to what we felt. We screamed when we were uncomfortable and smiled when we were happy. Soon after, when we started to navigate our bodies to explore the world around us, we learned from trial and error. Our thinking at this time was mostly based on memory and intuition.

When we went to elementary school, we were taught to do the logical thinking necessary for reading and writing and also the inductive reasoning that is needed for math. As we progressed to middle school, our logical reasoning continued and extended itself into our societal world. When we entered adolescence, we became more capable of thinking abstractly and manipulating ideas in our head for meeting the many challenges that faced us in this difficult time in our lives.

The way each one's thinking progresses depends on environmental factors and the kind of nurturing they receive. For many years, developmental psychologists were able to provide general stages for this progress and a timeline at which they would occur. But because of the many technological changes occurring in the twenty-first century, these stages are no longer applicable for us today.

Children are using digital devices at a very young age. As a result, their cognitive skills are accelerated. This isn't a bad thing, but we are noticing side effects. There is an increase in speed that is part of the digital world and it is often accompanied by sensory overload and greater stress and anxiety. We are pushed to move faster and in the flurry of activity, we become easily distracted and find it hard to slow down and focus our thoughts. Many are no longer taking the time to relax and read a book in preference to the excitement of surfing the internet.

It can be overwhelming to live in our fast-paced world if we do not have a way to deal with it. Fortunately we have been born with the basic intelligence we need to get us through it. We are also born with a built-in Witness that enables us to objectively observe everything we see in our outer and inner worlds. Our intellect is different than our witness, but working together, they give us all we need to manage our thoughts and enable us to have a peaceful and satisfying life.

In the words of contemporary shaman Odette Nightsky, "The inner witness is not addicted to any thought, it simply, neutrally observes without judgement...This is one of the most valuable skills that one can enhance and carry in their backpack of medicine tools."

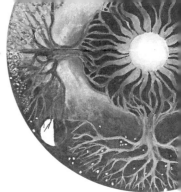

WHY STAY AWAKE FOR THE ADVENTURE?

"Some people feel the rain – others just get wet"
~ Bob Marley

We can be a lot more relaxed if we view our life as a sightseeing adventure at which it is impossible to fail. How can we fail at sightseeing unless we purposely close our eyes and sleep through the journey?

By staying awake and keeping our eyes open, there is much more potential for our journey to be an enjoyable one. Knowing how to observe can make it even better because it enables us to see more clearly and provides us with a greater view of things. This is true not only for times of pleasure, but for work and all the ordinary moments of daily living.

Being a good observer is important and useful for just about everybody. It is necessary for anyone who drives a vehicle. It is essential for all those in the workplace and spans the distance between those who are research scientists to game referees. To get a closer look for many varied purposes, we use microscopes, video replays and binoculars. In addition to that, many use elevated platforms from which to observe. These are crucial for Life Guards, Air Traffic Controllers and Forest Rangers for them to get the expansive view they need to do their jobs.

Observation towers are built in almost all of the major cities and vacation sites so that their visitors can enjoy a panoramic view of that location. The first was the Eiffel Tower that was built in Paris for the 1889 World's Fair. After that they began to pop up all over the world. Some more notable ones are The Space Needle in Seattle Washington, Washington Monument in Washington DC., the Gateway Arch in St. Louis, Missouri, and the Sky Tree in Tokyo Japan. Although not a tower but serving the same end, is the 443 foot Ferris wheel in England called The London Eye.

Although some of these serve the dual purpose as communication towers and were symbols of civic pride for the cities that built them, they were primarily designed to enhance visitor's ability to observe their surroundings in the greatest possible way.

To help us on our adventure we are pre-supplied with the useful senses of sight, sound, smell, taste and touch. They are quite amazing and when any of them is less than perfect, the others compensate so that we can still enjoy the richness of our experience.

Recently, my eldest son was at a bus station in Thailand working his way to the Bangkok Airport for his return trip to the United States. As in many places like this, Therapeutic Massage is offered for weary travelers. Being the weary traveler that he was, he entered the area that provides this service and noticed that all but one of several therapists was blind. My son was no stranger to massage therapy but never had it done by a blind person, so this is what he chose. When it was over he said it was the best massage he ever had.

Sometimes we move so fast to accomplish a task that we are unable to enjoy the process in the steps it takes to get there. We are often so busy with all that is on our agenda that we fail to notice anything but the strongest of sensations. We can feel the rush of adrenaline when we witness lightening in a thunderstorm but fail to be aware of how sweet it feels to be kissed by a gentle breeze or tickled by the touch of raindrops on our skin. We easily notice the smells that offend us but often don't stop long enough to put our nose close to a flower garden to appreciate the myriad of delicate aromas that it has to offer. When we eat too fast (or watch TV while we eat) we aren't aware of how much we've eaten or what it even tasted like.

Truly experiencing anything involves more than just 'going through the motions'. It requires that we slow down enough to become aware of what we are doing and noticing, or observing how it feels to be doing it.

Aside from being enjoyable, life on earth is difficult. From a Star Trek perspective, planet Earth could aptly be called 'The Boot Camp of the Universe'. It is full of stress and woe. To understand this, all we need do is turn on the television or radio and listen to a news report. Or we could walk out our door and get into traffic then go to a stressful workplace. All we need do is be a parent, hold down more than one job or be in a difficult relationship. It doesn't take much observing to see that struggle is all around us.

Sometimes we need help along the way. We are fortunate when we have friends that can give us encouragement and support. But if we don't, we can always find help through professional caregivers and guides. They are specially trained objective observers and can help get us through 'The worst of times'. The world would be a sorrier place without them.

But even the best friends or guides can only help us to a point and should always lead us toward being our own best teachers. If we depend too much on others to give us what we need, we become co-dependent and believe that we can only be happy if we have someone else to lean on or if circumstances go our way. 'Good luck with that'. We can never fully control what goes on around us. We can however, control the way we look at it. When we pause and observe our thoughts in an objective way, we are able to put things into a better perspective. We also give ourselves the opportunity to hear the gentle voice of our own inner guidance and become much more self-reliant.

WHAT DOES IT MEAN TO OBSERVE?

"To pay attention, this is our endless and proper work"
~Mary Oliver

To observe basically means to be aware or mindful. We do this by focusing our attention on that which is around us and within us. We listen and we look without judgment in order to see more clearly.

As any teacher or parent or anyone who knows a child will tell you that paying attention does not come naturally to them. It requires training and practice on their part and a lot of patience and creativity by those doing the training. All too often, children who can't pay attention are prescribed drugs for hyperactivity. But these come with serious side effects that have a negative impact on the rest of their lives. Fortunately, there is a trend today to bring a simple form of meditation into the classrooms of our schools to help them learn how to be more attentive. Children are not immune from the stress in the world. They often become hyperactive and anxious from what is happening around them. It has been found by clinical studies that meditation reduces levels of the stress hormone cortisol in the body. As a result, this lowers the feelings of tension in the person who is meditating.

When I would have students of any age do a meditative drawing called a Mandala in my classrooms, they would noticeably calm down and relax.

Meditative activities have been found to improve the student's level of attentiveness and improve their self-control. They have a positive influence on the whole atmosphere of the classroom as well and subsequently improve the mood of the teachers.

We adults also need to continually learn how to be more attentive. Who has not had an accident at some time in their life? Even though it clearly was not caused by another, our initial response is to blame someone or something else for causing it. Eventually we are faced with the fact that it might have been our fault for not *paying* better *attention*.

Looking and listening are essential for paying attention. Included in the required courses for the study of Counseling Psychology is always training in the Art of Listening. It is a necessary skill to have as a therapist in order to be able to pay the proper attention to their clients. Courses in listening may not be taught for all of those in fields of service, but it is certainly an important skill for anyone who works in a professional setting to be able to do their job in the best possible way.

Beyond that which is work related, knowing how to listen can be very helpful for improving our personal relationships as well. It is surprising to realize how poor many of us are at listening. We could probably find a way to take a course in the subject but can also improve this skill by talking less and not having a response ready before another person even completes their sentence. It has been said that we have two ears and only one mouth for a very good reason.

I must admit that I still would prefer to have someone hear what I have to say rather than listening to them. However, I know that by attentively listening to another, I can give them one of the greatest gifts they can receive. We all need to be heard and when we are, it is a healing thing that happens.

To go a step further, listening isn't always about doing it for others. It is also an incredible gift that we can give to ourselves. It is done by paying attention to what is known as our Intuition. It is defined as an *inner knowing* of something that just pops up inside of our head and resonates with our being. Some call it a *gut feeling*. Intuition is believed by neuroscience to be a physical function of the right side of the brain which is where creativity and inspiration live.

Many think of Intuition as the small still voice inside of us that can be a strong guiding force in our lives if we learn how to trust and act on it. Some are gifted with psychic abilities that aid the process but the majority of us need to gradually develop this function.

It can only be done by the use of trial and error and a lot of practice but it can be done because intuition exists in all of us. Albert Einstein relied on it often and encouraged others to do the same. He said: "The intuitive mind is a sacred gift and the rational mind is a faithful servant. We have created a society that honors the servant and has forgotten the gift". That being said, Intuition can help us tremendously but it is wise to use the rational mind along with it for discernment.

In an article from The National Catholic Review, Dec 9, 2014, Stephen Spielberg talks about trusting the Intuition for seeking our vocation or life's work. In his case, this is what led him to success as a Producer and Director in the Film Industry. He goes on to say that most of his movies also come as a result of listening to his intuition. He says that "it rarely shouts so we need to be ready to hear what it whispers in our ear".

Because it is such a quiet voice and there are so many distracting voices around us, it often repeats itself until we do notice it. It is similar to having a repeated dream. We have got to be grateful for the persistence in its efforts to get through to us.

* * *

Paying full attention is not an easy thing to do. It is much easier when we are focused on the present moment but we are constantly distracted by thoughts of the future or the past.

Looking toward the future is helpful for setting goals but other than that, we can't really do too much about it since it exists only in the imagination. We often become fearful with anticipation of the future but that doesn't serve us well. What serves us better is to set our goals and work with courage to achieve them while trusting the process it takes to get us there

If we don't dwell on it, the past can be more helpful to us. Looking back to review our accomplishments can be useful for bolstering a lagging confidence. Displaying credentials, photos and past achievements provides us with pride and great motivation to move forward. Looking at our past mistakes teaches us how to avoid them in the future. And observing former behaviors in an objective way can lead to understanding ourselves better in the present. This is what occurs in the process of psychotherapy.

In another way, objectively looking back over our lives when we are older can not only be an enjoyable past time but a therapeutic one as well. It is therapeutic because if we look over a large span of time, we are able to "connect the dots' of past events and see how they fit together into the bigger picture of who we are. It also helps us understand what our purpose has been in the world and gives us a better appreciation for being here. The 1946 movie, "It's a Wonderful Life", is a very good example of the benefits of such a backward glance.

Many people keep journals to record their feelings and experiences. When they look back on these, they have a wonderful way to review their past. Some write their memoirs which is therapeutic for the writer and often inspirational to those who read them.

For older adults who are unable or unmotivated to do this for themselves, friends or family members can be of great assistance by just asking them questions and recording the answers on tape or by writing. There are even bound journals available with pages that are headed with pertinent questions to guide the process. Children usually know their parents as the grownups that brought them into the world but seldom do they know much about the way these same parents were when they were growing up. To have this kind of knowledge about our elders after they are gone can be a priceless treasure.

Older adults in nursing homes can review their past with the help of professionals. It is referred to as "Life Review Therapy" and is credited to psychiatrist Dr. Robert Butler from his work with the geriatric population in the sixties. My closest neighbor is a beautiful example of a way to do Life Review all on his own. He is a 97 year old World War II Veteran. He lives alone and is blind and hard of hearing. He can only walk with the help of a walker and spends a lot of time in his easy chair. I often pay him visits and ask him how he is doing and he says, "I am fine and life is wonderful". When I ask him why he thinks life is wonderful and how he can sit so long by himself and not be bored, he says he daydreams about all of the past memories of his life "There are so many things to observe after all of these years and looking at them makes me happy and provides me with enough to do. His positive attitude is a constant inspiration to me.".

On the down side for many people, looking at the past can serve to feed depression and distract them from the present moment. For these, and for those suffering with PTSD, Life Review should be used very cautiously.

If we really want to be good at paying attention, it is essential that we learn how to live in the present moment. In truth, that is all we really have anyway. This is well put with the words of Author and Artist Jose Arquelles when he says:

All we have is NOW and NOW is all that will ever exist.

No one moment is more important than another. It may seem like we were born for the moments when we get what we want or have a great achievement. Sure, those feel really good but the feeling always fades and we are left with the ordinary steps in our process of living (and then wanting something more). It is wise and beneficial to focus our attention on these ordinary steps for each is significant and necessary in order to get to the next one. Each step in time is the moment we were born for.

Another thing we need for paying attention is a curiosity and openness to see what arises

When I start a work of art or begin any new project, I always put a little sign beside me that says: "Let's see what happens". I must have an idea of where I am headed and make suitable preparations to get there but I try to avoid a strict idea of how it will turn out. Sometimes, if I make a mistake in the process of my art, I discover that it leads me to a different and even better result.

Minister and author, Hugh Prather, said: "To live for results would be to sentence myself to continuous frustration. My only sure reward is in my actions and not from them." Our actions are the same as our process or journey. The results are the destination or goal. We do so much better if we don't push ourselves to arrive at the destination but relax into the process and allow it to unfold.

Recently, I offered to help one of my sons with a business that he was starting up by making cold calls to pertinent people to obtain market surveys. This was a scary thing to do. But to get through it, I decided to put myself in an objective position and be an observer of what was happening with each call. I pretended that I was watching a movie that I hadn't seen before and interested to see what would happen. I'm not saying that I didn't experience fear every time I made a new call but by stepping back and watching the process, I was able to face my fear and dial each number. I was able to obtain the calls that he needed and know this happened because I was observing the process rather than reacting to it. I could relax and engage those who dared to answer my calls in a friendly and non-threatening way and be in the moment without being overly stressed.

One of the things most needed for paying good attention is to observe without judgement.

There are basically two kinds of judgment making. There is the logical kind that we all must use as intelligent human beings in order to survive. It helps us with all of our life's choices, for everything from picking the best piece of fruit at the market to selecting our life's mate. The other kind of judgement is called criticism. There is constructive criticism which is given with the intent to help and involves the logical mind, but all too often, criticism is an emotional response and spoken to diminish another while subtly putting ourselves above them.

Critical judgement seems to come easy for we who were raised to think in dualistic terms. It is also strongly encouraged by competitive sports and Reality TV. But looking at things as if they are only right or wrong, only good or bad or only black and white, prevents us from seeing all the details and shades in between. It prevents us from being open to a more complete picture. Since we can only see the part of the picture that is revealed to us at any given time, we need to 'hold the reins' and guard against jumping to conclusions. Besides it serves our humility to realize that we don't know all things.

In order to see more clearly, we need to curb our tendencies to judge one another. We are all part of the same human family and as in all families we are each different and have our own individual tastes and make our own particular choices. And unless we have an extraordinary imagination or have the gifts of an empath, we don't really know what it's like to walk in another's shoes so we can never really know enough to make a valid criticism about anyone.

It is helpful to remember the words of the Ancient Roman philosopher Philo of Alexandria who said "Be kind, for every one you meet is fighting a great battle".

Equally as important, we need to keep ourselves from making comparisons to others because it always blocks our ability to understand and love them and to love ourselves as well. Each of us is unique with our own gifts and abilities. No two are perfectly alike (not even identical twins) and no other can do what we do in the way that only we can do it. In her book "Appearances" Rusty Berkus states:

There is no one to compare yourself to,
and no one to compete with.
There never was.
When the Rose and the Lotus
are side by side,
is one more beautiful than the other?

What we all really need from each other are words of encouragement to help us remain strong and persevere through the many challenges that Life continually offers.

The need to observe without judgement has to apply first and foremost to ourselves.

As well as having an 'Inner Witness', we all seem to have a well-functioning 'Inner Critic'. If we have experienced a lot of criticism in our lives, our inner critic is usually in 'overdrive' and it is hard for us to think well of ourselves. We can be full of self-doubt and low self-esteem. Sometimes we aren't even aware of the self-criticism and negative babble that goes on in our heads. But if we remain unaware, it just serves to perpetuate our self-loathing and keeps us stuck in a false view of ourselves.

The truth is, at any given time, we are complete and whole just as we are.

We don't need to add anything to ourselves to be better and are always worthy to be loved.

Alongside of our inner critic, we will often have those around us suggesting that we aren't good enough. There are pressures from society to have us look and act a certain way if we want to be accepted. We are graded by teachers that convey a need for improvement if our scores are low, even though we have done the best we could. Churches sometimes label us as guilty at the 'get go' and in need of reform. But this is all part of the conditioning that we must look at and rethink.

We need to understand that we are intrinsically good enough. We are deserving of love at all times regardless of what is happening around us. But we can't always count on getting this love from outside ourselves. We can and must give it to ourselves because ultimately, we are the loving partner that we need the most. *Loving and approving of ourselves is where our happiness lies.*

To become more proficient in loving ourselves, we need to practice it on a daily basis. To start with, we could take just one day and decide that whatever comes up in our outer and inner worlds will be observed objectively and seen as a chance to be patient and kind to ourselves all that day long. If we do this consistently, it will become a habit. We will become easier for ourselves to live with and when we are kinder to ourselves we naturally are kinder to others. Having a regular practice of meditation and doing it without self-judgement, is like giving ourselves a daily cup of love and turning this act of kindness into a way of life.

Watercolor   Stacey Hoffer Weckstein 2011

"Be kinder to yourself than you think you should"
~Zen Teacher Cheri Huber

WHAT IS MEDITATION?

"If you can breathe you can meditate"
~ Sharon Salzburg

The most refined form of observation is through the practice of meditation.

Meditation is not a religion and is not in conflict with religion. It is however, different from it. Religion is practiced in a social context to support one's faith and beliefs. Although meditation can, and is encouraged to be done in groups, its focus is more individual and its goal is to move inward to find peace and develop a more personal and experiential relationship with God.

Meditation is also encouraged in all of the major religions of the world through their sacred writings. In many of these texts, the word *meditate* is used the same as *prayer, contemplation* or mindfulness, even though there are differences specific to each of these words. Prayer generally involves supplication, contemplation is about thinking, and mindfulness is the same as observing. All of them however, can be included in the broadest context of the word meditation.

For Christianity, references to meditation appear throughout the Old and New Testaments of the Bible. In the book of Joshua 1:8 (NRSV) it is written "This book of the law shall not depart out of your mouth; you shall meditate on it day and night so that you may be careful to act in accordance with it. For then you shall make your way prosperous, and then you shall be successful." In Paul's letter to the Philippians 4:8, he says "Finally brethren, whatever is true, whatever is honorable, whatever is right, whatever is pure, whatever is lovely, whatever is of good repute, if there is any excellence and if anything worthy of praise, think upon (contemplate) these things." The word observe is used in Matthew 6:27-29 "Who of you by being worried can add a single hour to his life? And why are you worried about clothing? Observe how the lilies of the field grow; they do not toil nor do they spin, yet I say to you that not even Solomon in all his glory clothes himself like one of these." On more than one occasion, Jesus was noticed going off by himself to pray and meditate and He encouraged his followers to do the same. And the life of mystics and all those in monastic communities revolve around the practice of meditation through song and prayer and contemplation.

But beyond the walls of monasteries there is much encouragement and support for today's Christians to meditate and lead a more spiritual life. Fr. Thomas Keating introduced "Centering Prayer' as a form of Christian meditation. Fr. Richard Rohr provides generous support for contemplative living through his writing and teachings. And Fr. Edward Hays has inspired many with his books and Art that integrate ancient wisdom into the fabric of modern day Christianity.

Hospitals are providing classes in meditation to help their patients deal with depression, anxiety and pain. Corporations are having them to help employees to combat stress in the workplace. Colleges are providing instruction in meditation for their students and those in the community who want to attend. They are offered in Churches and even taught to police officers and those in the Military to improve mental performance under the stress and strain of their service. There are also Meditation Centers that provide specialized training on the subject from people of all faiths and beliefs. If these are not readily accessible, there are many excellent teachers available on the internet.

Much of the meditation that is practiced in the Western World today is derived from Buddhism. Their practices are centered on the Four Noble Truths which speak of life as suffering and the way to end that suffering through the Eightfold Path of Right Living. Their focus is on finding 'stillness within', in order to be able to move with ease in the ever changing and impermanent world in which we live. The ultimate goal of their practices is to attain Enlightenment. This is believed to be achieved through the development of wisdom, morality and meditation.

For Islam, the Koran stresses meditation and contemplation throughout all of its 114 chapters. The required prayers that Muslims do five times a day are similar to meditation because of their purpose of focusing the mind on God. Sufism, which is the mystical element of Islam, and founded by Jalal ad-Din Muhammad Rumi, has practices that are even more synonymous with regular meditation. Also, the Sufi Whirling Dervishes do an active meditation by dancing in circles in order to focus the mind on God. These have been modified and danced by people of all faiths in countries all over the world. They are called 'Dances of International Peace'.

The Hindu religion of India is best known as the source of the meditative practice of Yoga which is a favorite form of exercise by many Western Americans. Yoga combines physical postures, breathing techniques, and meditation. The physical postures are helpful in reducing pain and improving flexibility of the muscles and joints. Breathing techniques serve to increase the body's circulation and helps our concentration and our ability to focus. The meditation at the end of the sessions is provided to offer relaxation, invaluable for relieving stress in our fast paced world.

In Judaism, meditation was the primary tool used by the ancient prophets and leaders of Israel, such as Moses and King David, to receive divine communication and guidance. Today, meditation is considered an essential ingredient in Jewish services when chanting verses from the psalms or Torah or saying prayers. Kabbalah, which is the mystical branch of Judaism, contains many kinds of meditative practices for uniting one's soul with God.

In all forms of mysticism, meditation is the way that beliefs are internalized and made to bring the believer to the fullness of their faith.

The Indigenous people in the Americas and those in other places in the world, do not consider themselves as religions but their understanding of the sacredness of the earth and their connection to the 'Great Spirit – Great Mystery' are integral to their way of living. They have many prayerful rituals and ceremonies to support their daily living and to mark special occasions in their lives. These utilize dancing, drumming and chanting and some involve opening to silence and going within for rituals such as the Sweat Lodge, Vision Quest, Peyote and Sundance Ceremonies.

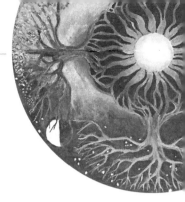

HOW DO WE GET STARTED?

"Purge your mind of Fear and Trust Yourself"
~ Remo Williams, the Journey Begins

In my early adulthood, I had the unique experience of belonging to a religious community of nuns for five years. On entering, we were required to spend three years of formative training as Novices. During this time we learned the spiritual practices of our founders and did concentrated studies in Scripture and Theology. We also took related college classes to prepare us to work as teachers, nurses and in other fields of service. After these three years we were offered to take temporary vows of Poverty, Chastity and Obedience before going to our assigned places to live and work.

It was the Sixties and while many young people in the country were engaged in a *Sexual Revolution*, I was wearing long black robes and committed to a penitential life-style. We had strict rules to follow that made convent-living very challenging. One of my brothers visited me there shortly after completing Boot Camp in the Marines and said he thought I had chosen a more disciplined path than he had. He may have been right because even though I had the love and support of the other Sisters to carry me through, I found it too difficult to persevere as a Nun. One of the main reasons for this was that I was an artist and entered the Novitiate with two years of training in that field. I was given some opportunities to use my creative talents, for which I was very grateful. For the most part however, I felt inhibited by the rules of obedience and the requirements to conform, so I decided to turn in my robes and breviary and left before taking final vows.

It took courage to return to the world after being sheltered from it for five years. I left in need of some therapy but also was armed with good practices to help me lead a peaceful and God centered life. One of them was that of meditating. We would arise at 5:20 am, kiss the floor and after getting dressed under our nightgowns, would go to the chapel to meditate and pray before Daily Mass. Starting the day this way was a good habit to develop (no pun intended). A good breakfast is important but feeding the Soul in the morning is what really gets us through the day.

Another practice was that of doing daily spiritual reading. I continue that practice to this day and it continues to sustain the awareness of the spiritual nature within me.

Also, each year, we would make a week long silent retreat. Other than not working quite as hard during that week, and having some special spiritual speakers, we went about business as usual except for not being allowed to talk. It's amazing how many ways there are to communicate without talking. It was actually not bad however and the silence was a good way to help quiet the mind and bring better focus to the Inner Self which is really what meditation is all about.

My experience was not a typical way to get started on the path of meditation. Most come by it in more subtle ways. Some may be inspired to meditate by the witness of a saintly person like Mother Theresa. We could be influenced by the example of a friend, a quiet neighbor who lives a peaceful and authentic life, or a criminal in prison using an awareness practice to calm their mind and bring them inner peace. It could come from seeing a movie like "Kung Foo Panda" or hearing a song by the Beatles. For some it will hopefully come from reading this book.

The inspiration to go deeper can come from any place and at any time. It is a call to explore our minds and bring greater awareness to our lives. It is an invitation that is worthy to accept.

Physical work is about tending to the needs of our external world. It is necessary and important if we intend to survive. Meditation is about tending to the needs of our internal world and is just as important if we want to survive with awareness and peace. Although it looks like we are doing nothing, it is definitely not a passive activity. During this process, we are nurturing a neglected part of ourselves that really needs our attention.

I'm reminded of the story about the Native American elder who was speaking to his grandchild and saying: "I have two wolves fighting in my heart. One wolf is vengeful, fearful, envious, resentful, and deceitful. The other wolf is loving, compassionate, generous, truthful, and serene." The grandchild asks which wolf will win the fight. The elder answers, "The one I feed."

For those who want to try a sitting meditation on their own:

* First of all, decide on a time that you can give yourself at least five or ten quiet minutes a day.
* Then find a spot where you are able to sit comfortably with your spine as straight as possible.
* Close your eyes or keep them slightly open and focused on one single spot ahead of you.
* Then follow your breath as it comes in and out of your nostrils.
* Do this for as long as you are able and be as still as you possibly can.
* When finished, rise up, stretch out and take your 'awareness practice' into the unfolding day.

First of all, decide on a time that you can give yourself at least five or ten quiet minutes a day.

For very active people this might be the most difficult thing because it requires slowing down enough to come to a complete stop.

When choosing a time, mornings are good but any time and place where you can be alone without distraction is best. Many people find it helpful to start and finish their day with sitting.

It is very helpful to make a schedule for yourself so that you can be sure to fit these few precious moments into your day.

Then, find a spot where you are able to sit comfortably. It doesn't have to be on a cushion on the floor. It can be in a chair or even on a bench. Wherever you choose, ***sit with your spine as straight as possible.*** Circulation of blood to the brain is better in that position. And after doing this for a while, you might notice that your posture and alertness will improve and you might not need as many trips to the chiropractor.

You can close your eyes or keep them slightly open and focused on one single spot ahead of you and then, follow your breath as it comes in and out of your nostrils.

The breath is the most reliable friend we have to take us through it all.

While you are doing this, many thoughts will arise to distract you. It's been estimated that we can have as many as two to three thousand thoughts in one hour's time. While we are awake, we have a tremendous amount of fast speed information that is bombarding us from all of the electronics that we live with. It is so necessary that we have a way to find calm in this storm of information. If we don't find a way to center the mind and bring it to a point of stillness, we are apt to self-destruct from overload.

The mind has been referred to as being like a monkey who is always jumping around from one thing to another. We can see this happening in our dreams. We can be in one location with people doing one thing and instantly find ourselves all alone and in another place doing something entirely different. It is so empowering to have a lucid dream as when you realize in your sleep that you are actually dreaming. You can be in grave danger and when the thought occurs to you that you are dreaming, you are able to magically change the situation and save yourself from harm. (It can work the same way in our waking hours if we understand that our reality is only a dream-like picture of our perceptions. If we change our perceptions, we also change our reality.)

Because our thoughts are so active, they need to be brought under control. In essence, we are taming our monkey-minds when we meditate. We do this by briefly acknowledging the presence of the thought and then letting it go. It is helpful to see the thoughts like clouds passing by in the sky and after they move on, you return your attention again to the breath. . This is the basic challenge of meditation and needs to be done over and over again. It does get easier with practice.

Do this for as long as you are able and be as still as possible.

We don't start out sitting for long periods of time but as we get more comfortable with the process it becomes easier to extend our time. You will also notice that the longer you meditate the greater will be your rewards. At the beginning of most sessions, it might feel that your mind is like a muddy lake. The longer you sit, the mud seems to settle to the bottom and the lake becomes beautifully clear and calm.

Meditation offers us the chance to practice 'being in what is'. Doing this over time helps to remove our resistance to discomfort and strengthens our ability to persevere.

Every session is different from the other, and they all won't be wonderful but **when we think we have failed, it is just an opportunity to show extra love to ourselves.**

Keep in mind that nobody is perfect in keeping a daily practice (except perhaps the Pope or the Dali Lama and those in monastic communities) however, we will find that the more consistently meditation is done, the more benefits we will derive from it, even if it's not for a long period each time. And keep in mind that **there is great power in repetition.**

Repetition is also the way we are able to form new patterns. Before we consciously start to observe and be aware of ourselves, most of our thoughts and actions occur out of habitual pattern. If we don't want to be a slave to those patterns, we can change them. The best way to change a habit is to start a new one and the only way to accomplish that is by repetition. Forming a new habit is always more difficult in the beginning but by taking consistent small steps one after the other we will go forward in the desired direction and accomplish our goal.

The computer scientist Matt Cutts, presents a short but powerful idea on a 'Ted Talk' about doing something new for 30 days and guarantees that we can create a new habit in just that amount of time.

For some things, it takes less time. I was in the habit of drinking coffee in the morning and decided to see if I could break that habit by drinking tea. I found I like tea but then decided to switch back to coffee when I felt I was becoming a slave to tea. It might sound insignificant but it gave me confidence and a sense of power in being able to make changes in these small ways.

When finished, rise up, stretch out and take your 'awareness practice' into the unfolding day.

After a meditation period is over, you will most likely feel stiff from sitting in one position for an extended time. It's advisable to stretch a bit and move your muscle to restore your flexibility. If you are meditating alone, this might be a good time to fit exercise into your schedule but whatever it is that you do afterward, try to bring the same awareness of yourself into it as you did when you were sitting. This is the ultimate purpose of a meditation practice, which is to bring awareness into your unfolding day.

The Wisdom Teacher Krishnamurti said of Real meditation that: "It is not a matter of sitting cross-legged in a corner with your eyes shut or standing on your head or whatever it is you do. To meditate is to be completely aware as you are walking, as you are riding in the bus, as you are working in your office or in your kitchen- completely aware of the words you use, the gestures you make, the manner of your talk, the way you eat, and how you push people around. To be choicelessly aware of everything about you and within your Self, is meditation".

Being completely aware is quite a large order to fill for any of us but it does present a goal that we can slowly work toward.Doing a regular sitting practice at the start, makes the kind of awareness that Krishnamurti talks about, much more achievable.

His words suggest that there are countless ways to move closer to that goal. As long as we are being observant of ourselves and our surroundings, we can always be meditating. This is good news for the busier and more active among us who can start to meditate with a walk in Nature, while they are getting a massage or soaking in a tub. They can be exercising, working in a garden, having a cup of tea, moving their bodies to music, or doing a spontaneous drawing or painting. Over the years, working with the art form of the Mandala has been one of my favorite ways to meditate.

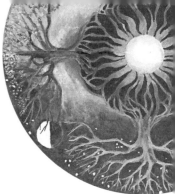

WHAT IS A MANDALA ANYWAY?

*"The Mandala signifies the wholeness of the self. . .or to put
in mythic terms, the divinity incarnate in man"*
~ Carl Jung

Mandala is a Sanskrit word meaning "Sacred Circle". The circle is a symbol of continuity and wholeness. It has been used by people of all cultures as a way to sanctify space and connect to their Source. It appears as an art form throughout ancient and modern times in such examples as the sand paintings of the Tibetan Buddhists and the Navaho Indians in America. It was used in the design of the layouts of primitive villages and in the city plan for Washington D.C. You can see this symbolic circle in Celtic mandalas with their intricate designs of unbroken lines and the Rose Window in the Cathedral of Notre Dame. They appear in the Medicine Wheels of the Lakota Sioux and the ancient Aztec calendar called the Sun Stone.

Oglala Sioux Indian Black Elk explains the Mandala with these words:

"Everything the Power of the World does is done in a circle. The sky is round, and I have heard that the earth is round like a ball, and so are all the stars. The wind, in its greatest power, whirls. Birds make their nests in circles, for theirs is the same religion as ours. The Sun comes forth and goes down again in a circle. The Moon does the same, and both are round. Even the seasons form a great circle in their changing, and always come back to where they were. The life of man is a circle from childhood to childhood, and so it is in everything where power moves. Our tepees were round like the nests of birds, and these were always set in a circle, the nation's hoop, a nest of many nests, where the Great Spirit meant for us to hatch our children."

In his Intergalactic Mandala called "The Divine Presence" Father Edward Hays illustrates that "All life flows out from the Divine Center and flows back again. As the seasons flow naturally from one to another, as night gives birth to day, so life rises from death according to the Eternal Promise."

Because the Mandala defines the biological principal that all things grow out of their own center and are interconnected with everything else that exists, we can see them all around us in the way things grow in nature. Just look at a blooming flower, observe the cross section of a tree, or look at the inside of a piece of fruit or a vegetable.

In its simplest approach, we can arrange any objects in the shape of a circle and be able to call it a mandala as long as it has a noticeable center. We can create mandalas by using flowers, stones, shoes, pictures or even food. Some can be free formed and others can be symmetrical. We can also draw or paint mandalas with art materials.

Here are some simple instructions for making a spontaneous one on paper.

1. Draw a circle on paper with a pencil by tracing around a plate or circular object.

2. Use oil pastel, chalks, marker or colored pencils.

   Select any color that appeals to you and make a mark in the center of the circle.

3. Allow the mark to grow spontaneously.

   Withhold judgement. You cannot do it incorrectly.

4. The drawing can be abstract or pictorial and the colors or shapes can be changed at any time.

5. The outside pencil line should not be regarded as a boundary.

6. When finished, sign and date and write any comments you wish.

7. Place them where you can see them frequently and be open to what they have to say.

This is an example of one that followed the previous instructions. After drawing the circle, a scribble drawing was done starting from the center and then selected shapes were filled in with color. This is a fun and easy mandala to do and could possibly reveal to its artist that even a chaotic mind can be beautiful.

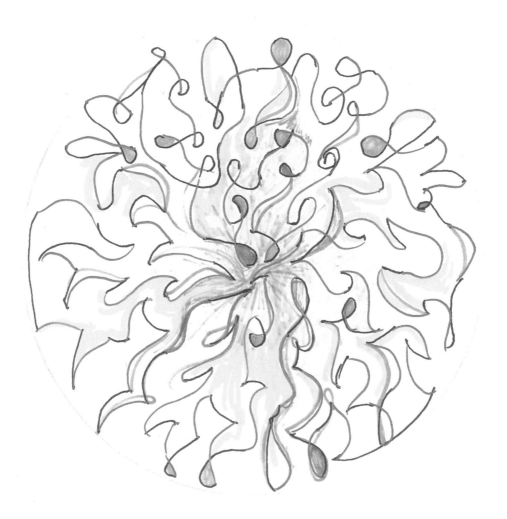

Mandalas don't always need to be drawn in a circle. (A square can also be considered as the boundary for a Mandala) A circle provides a safe place to work within but you can get this same sense of containment while doing one on graph paper. This was started in the middle square and worked out from there. It is a good way to relax when you need one.

Mandalas can also be done as a vehicle for self-expression. You can keep a sketch book journal of them as a safe way to externalize your feelings. Feelings are always better out instead of being stuffed within and when you are finished with your drawing, you will have an image to provide you with a hint of what is going on inside of your head.

Swiss psychologist Carl Jung suggested that a spontaneous drawing of a mandala represented a picture of the unconscious mind that could serve as a quiet teacher of self-awareness. He believed that interpreting what the colors, shapes and objects in a drawing mean to us, we can decipher the coded message that appears.

Art therapists often have their clients draw a mandala to be used as an assessment tool when developing their treatment plans. They also use mandala making as part of their treatment plan as well.

Joan Kellogg, Judith Cornell, and Susanne Fincher are all authors and artists that have been very instrumental in bringing the use of mandala making into mainstream psychology and introducing it to the present Western world at large. To pursue an interest in learning more about the Mandala, I would recommend starting with any one of these authors.

There are computer programs to help us generate symmetrical mandalas. These can be printed and put where we can see them frequently to help us calm and center our mind. They can also be used to look at as a focus point when doing sitting meditation. You can use a drawing of a mandala that you have made yourself for the same purpose. There are many mandala coloring books available to buy and use the finished pages in the same way. Also, free mandalas are available on various web sites for downloading and printing. A couple of these have been included at the end of this chapter.

Just the act of coloring a mandala has proved to be a valid and therapeutic form of meditation for many. For the active person, it is a wonderful way of slowing down and relaxing.

Another way of doing an active meditation is to Dance a Mandala.

Most meditative dancing is done in the form of a circle. Almost all cultures have done them as a way of connecting with each other and strengthening community life. Some examples of these are the early folk dances done in Eastern European countries. For modern day Slovaks, a

"Wedding Dance" is still performed at the end of the reception. After each guest has danced individually with the bride, they form a close circle around her that her new husband has to break through in order to collect his bride and carry her off to the Honeymoon.

Jewish people do a circle dance called Hora for rituals and to celebrate joyous occasions. This is done to the music, Hava Nagila which means, 'Let us rejoice'.

The Greeks do a dance called Syrtos. It has many variations depending on the location in which it is done but occurs in a circle or semi-circle and is characterized by moving in a counterclockwise direction while linked together by a handkerchief or by holding hands, wrists or shoulders.

Dance has always been an integral part of African Society and still remains so today. Usually the dances are done to beautiful rhythmic music for ceremonies and celebrations or just for fun. Some Ritual round dances are done with the participants wearing Masks in order to connect to the Gods their costumes represent.

Native Americans do circle dances to chants. Many are done around a fire like the Chickasaw Nation's 'Stomp Dance'. Some tribes do a dance to acknowledge the sacredness of the Cardinal Directions of East, West, South, and North. The Sioux Nation acknowledges 7 sacred directions. They dance to the main four and add prayers to Father Sky, Mother Earth and the sacred place within where the Great Spirit- Great Mystery dwells.

We can see the influence of all of these dances in the games that children play today. Who has not played 'Ring around the Rosy' or 'Here we go round the Mulberry Bush'. It is still a custom in some places for children to hold and weave a ribbon while they dance around a pole for a May Day celebration. Most of these circle dances are done in groups but we can create one for ourselves alone and use music of our choosing to dance our own private Mandala.

Meditating for the active person can also be done by walking, practicing Tai Chi, floating on water, listening to music, star gazing, looking at the paintings of artists, or any number of other slow paced activities.

Walking a Labyrinth is a wonderful moving meditation.

A Labyrinth is a circular patterned path used for quieting the mind and helping it to go inward. Its path is designed so that the walker moves back and forth across the circle through repeated curves that end up in the center. These are commonly found near churches or at retreat centers but many design and place them in their private gardens for their own personal use. For more temporary ones, some make them in the sand at the beach or in the winter snow.

A **walking** meditation can be done anywhere, but if you are up for a challenge, try walking so slowly that you can feel every part of the sole of your feet as it touches down on the earth and lifts off of it again. Notice how it feels when it is in the air and your other foot has to compensate to balance your body. Do this so slowly that you can only make 6 or 7 steps in one minute. It is great to do it in your bare feet on grass.

Tai Chi is an offspring of Martial arts and has developed into a mindful, low impact form of exercise that is meant to improve the circulation of Chi or life energy within the body. It involves grounding the feet to the earth and making slow, graceful and deliberate movements for the purpose for increasing body awareness and promoting relaxation. It can be done by people of any age and is best started under the guidance of a teacher. Classes are usually available in most communities. It is a beautiful meditation in motion.

Some of our best moments of relaxation can come from **Floating** on our back on water. In less buoyant moments, a small swimming raft can help. There is something wonderful about yielding the body to the water and feeling completely supported by it. It gives us a chance to be totally relaxed and free of striving. An interesting experience in floating can be had in a **Float tank.** They are also called Sensory Deprivation Tanks. These tanks are capsules that look similar to a large egg and contain a warm shallow pool of dense salt water. It is light and sound proof and big enough for one person to use at a time. Floating this way slows down all of the body's functions and has numerous physical and mental benefits. There are only a few of these in the world however and you would be fortunate not to have to travel to find one. There is presently a Tank in Shadyside Pittsburgh in Western Pennsylvania. Others can be found in Montana, Kentucky, Colorado, Oregon, Canada, India, New Zealand and Australia.

Music is a good background for any meditation but it can also be used as a focus for the same. This is done by giving our full attention to it and allowing our self to feel it without judgement. If we become distracted, we bring our attention back to the music as we do to the breath in sitting meditation. It is possible to buy music for this kind of practice and some include guided meditations as a part of them.

Stargazing is a meditative experience that can be had by anyone in any place except for those in the Poles at the time of the midnight sun. Many find it helpful to lay on the ground and let their body's relax while Stargazing. Others enjoy a closer look through a telescope but they both provide the opportunity for expanding the mind to observe its greater possibilities.

Making art can be a meditation but ***viewing art can be a meditative experience*** as well. To stand or sit silently in front of an art piece and observe it without doing too much thinking enables us to feel the energy of the piece and even connect with the artist who created it.

"Starry Night" 2′5″x3′0″   Vincent Van Gogh 1889

Do some art therapy today. Grab some pencils or crayons to color and
even elaborate on the mandala above to help you to relax.

Creating or coloring a mandala can help us to center and calm our mind.

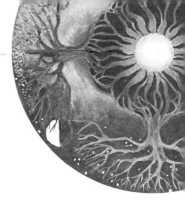

HOW DOES MEDITATION BENEFIT THE BODY?

"I praise you because I am fearfully and wonderfully made"
~ Psalm 139:14

What astounding bodies we have been given to work with. Even though they aren't perfect and often have serious limitations and problems, they endure a lot and work very hard for us, even when we're tired. It's important to acknowledge them and thank them for all they do. They hold us together in a well-organized package and have wonderful moving parts that take us from one place to another. Our bodies contain a heart that consistently pumps and circulates our blood and a brain that's available for solving problems and helping to direct our choices.

We need to be grateful for our bodies even if they don't look or work as well as somebody else's. It is especially important to honor them for hosting our sacred Spirit and being willing to follow its lead.

Being in our bodies is a temporary thing but while we are in them we must show them as much kindness and respect as possible if we want them to continue to do their valuable work for us.

One of the best ways we can show our bodies kindness is by maintaining them as well as we can and keeping them moving and engaged in activity as much as we are able. Equally as important is how we nourish them. We must first give them good food and drinks and secondly avoid the food and drinks that will harm them. This is no small challenge today because we are so dependent on others to grow and provide our food and are never quite sure about how it was grown and what has been added to it. Actress Meryl Streep has been quoted as saying "It's bizarre that the produce manager is more important to my children's health than the pediatrician".

Fortunately, we aren't left totally at a loss because of the wonderful organic farmers that make a pure grade of food available to us and because of the fact that we can make our own gardens if we have the time and space. It is also encouraging that we have many Holistic professionals to help direct us along this challenging path of nutrition.

After we maintain our bodies with good nutrition and exercise, they may still come down with problems and diseases. This is because we are more than bodies moving around like well-maintained robots without feelings. And many of the physical problems we have come from emotional stress and our inability to manage it.

According to WebMD, stress can be the cause of many physical conditions such as heart disease, asthma, obesity, diabetes, stomach ulcers, headaches, depression, anxiety, and insomnia to name a few.

Stress is unavoidable in daily living. For one thing, because of the fact that life is not permanent, it is always changing and as much as we would like, we can't pin it down and hold it still.

Change is a number one Stressor. These changes are often unpredictable. Just look at the weather and all that it presents. The physical changes that come with the growth of our bodies and the effects it encounters from its environment can be a major stressor. Our relationships are constantly changing because the people in them are changing as well. Losing what we love is at the top of the list of stressors, whether it is another person, a pet, a job, a home, or anything that we cherish.

Personal, national and international disasters are occurring every minute and because of modern technology, we get to hear about them, even as they are happening. There is a constant bombardment of distractions coming at us from text messages, emails and pings from our digital calendars. TV programming and even the ads are designed to create stress by their focus on speed, competition and presenting the neediest and worst side of human nature.

Life can be overwhelming at times. We must be able to find a place of stillness within ourselves

In order to survive. One good way to start is to turn off all electronic input for a while. Another is to get outdoors and be with nature. If those aren't possible and even if you are in a busy noisy place, you can find sanctuary by briefly closing your eyes and allowing a long deep breath to move you to the center of yourself.. A full breath and one thought can immediately take you there. If you find this pleasant, do return trips until you feel calm enough to open your eyes. This is like an instant meditation and does wonders to relieve stress and restore your sanity.

To help visualize going to this peaceful sanctuary, you can compare it to the using of a potter's wheel. Initially, a lump of clay has to be thrown in the center of the wheel before it is made to spin. Then when the wheel starts to turn, the lump is held firmly by both hands in the center so that it doesn't wobble or move at all while the outside of the wheel spins at high speed. The positioning of the clay is crucial to the rest of the process. If it is even a little off center the clay will wobble and collapse as a vessel is being formed. ***We are the clay and our peace depends on being centered and still as the world spins wildly around us.***

This kind of mini-retreat and all forms of meditation are the best defense against stress and can improve many of the problems that are caused by it. When we take the time to slow down and pay conscious attention to our breath, we are able to experience how well it can serve us. We don't realize how often in a day our breath is so shallow that we are barely breathing at all. We might automatically take a big gulp of air to catch up with what we're lacking. Stress can slow down our breathing and almost bring it to a halt and after noticing that we are able to restart our engine, so to speak. And breathing fully does wonders to help us to RELAX.

NOW - TAKE A DEEP BREATH – LET IT OUT SLOWLY - and notice how your body feels. If one breath doesn't slow you down, lower your shoulders and do it again.

Meditating regularly can improve our health in many ways. It is not to be considered as a replacement for medical treatment but in most cases can truly enhance it.

Recently, after undergoing surgery for a total hip replacement, my body systems became abnormal and out of balance. All of the manageable conditions I had going into surgery became unmanageable from the trauma to my body. I found myself in a heightened state of stress which only intensified my problems. Medication, meditation and gentle alternative therapies helped to alleviate my stress and slowly brought me back into balance again.

Meditation is recommended by many health care professionals for the management of pain. Nobody likes pain. We instinctively try to avoid it but when it can't be avoided, meditation can help us to deal with it.

For example, when we are sitting and notice a small thing like an itch, we can immediately scratch it or we can be with the sensation and objectively observe it as it comes and goes. If it doesn't go, we can breathe into it and more or less become one with it. It's interesting to notice that when you are not resisting any sensation it becomes much less in intensity. It involves an act of surrender and this yielding relaxes us to the point that we can be with it a lot easier.

This approach also involves a willingness to move toward pain rather than running away from it. There is a well-known story about the founder of Naropa University, Chogyam Trungpa when he was going to a meeting at a friend's house with a group of people and they encountered a charging dog that had broken loose from its containment and was running toward them with bared teeth. Chogyam told the group to stand still and he ran toward the charging dog as fast as he could. The dog became so confused that it stopped and ran in the opposite direction. It can sometimes work the same way with pain if we choose not to flee from it.

It is also not the best choice to run from pain and suffering because there is great value in it for us. We don't always see its value while we are moving through it but it eventually reveal itself.

When I look back at what can be described as the worst times of my life, they have turned out to be the most meaningful in terms of my growth in wisdom and maturity. If we don't let it get the best of us, struggling through pain and suffering can then be seen as a gift to strengthen us.

According to 'The Art of Living Organization", there are various other ways in which meditation can benefit our health. They have found that meditating ten minutes two times a day can reduce blood pressure after 12 weeks. For some this works even better than medication. It increases serotonin production that helps to improve our mood. It lowers levels of blood lactate that reduces the frequency of anxiety attacks. Meditating regularly can also help to improve our immune system and as we gain inner strength from its practice, our energy increases.

Meditation can help insomnia because its process reduces the stress hormone cortisol and increases the relaxation hormone oxytocin in our bodies. In a relaxed state, it is easier for both our body and our mind to slow down. Also the process requires that we make a conscious decision to focus on our breath. Since it is impossible to have two different thoughts at the same time, when we think   about breathing, we can effectively replace the racing and worrisome thoughts with a single focused one and fall asleep more easily.

Having a meditation practice can also enhance the performance of athletes. For many professionals, sports psychologists use mental skill training to develop concentration and stress control. This skill training often includes techniques that are very similar to meditation for body awareness and relaxation. They influence confidence and self-esteem and are quite successful in helping athletes to achieve their goals.

Any sport activity that requires the concentrated focus of attention is improved from the skills learned in the practice of meditation.

To help us take care of our bodies we have Health Care professionals to rely on but quite often we can help ourselves. If we have a condition that we know is not life threatening, we can observe it for a while and allow our body's own wisdom to reveal itself through our intuition so that we don't need to visit a doctor for all of our answers.

Taking good care of our bodies also means that sometimes we need to put ourselves first. Anybody who has flown on a plane has heard the instruction that if you have a child and there is need to use oxygen we need to put the mask on ourselves first. If we don't do this, the child won't be able to be helped at all.

We have all heard that it is better to give than to receive but that does not apply to everything. At times when we are asked to help another and it would put us to a disadvantage, we need to be able to say "No, I'm sorry but I'm unable to help you at this time", and not feel guilty about it. We really don't need to make sacrifices to prove that we are good. And sometimes when we do, we end up being angry at ourselves and resenting the person who asked. It is not a selfish thing to put ourselves first. It is actually required. We are told on good authority 'to love our neighbor as we love our self'.

Here are words to consider from a Native Tribal Community: Dear One, if I asked you to name all the things you love, how long would it take you to mention yourself?

Some Ideas for Promoting Self Love

Write a love note in a card and send it to yourself.

If you do something stupid, refrain from calling yourself a name.
Instead say, "It's okay Honey, everybody makes mistakes".

Write a list of everything you have accomplished in the day so far.
Start with the fact that you got out of bed in the morning.

Put your arms around you and give yourself a big hug.

Treat yourself to a little gift.

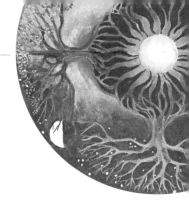

HOW DOES MEDITATION BENEFIT THE MIND?

"Everything changes once we identify with being the
witness to the story instead of the actor in it"
~ Ram Dass

We all want to be happy. Many of us think that if we have enough money and the right person to love that this will give it to us. It doesn't. How often have we gotten what we want and felt happy about it for a while then found that we want something different shortly afterwards. Happiness, like pleasure, is an emotion that is short lived. It is wiser to seek after something more lasting that won't come and go so predictably.

Paul of Tarsus in his letter to the Philippians, speaks highly of contentment as a worthy pursuit and one that can be achieved at any moment in time. He wrote: "I know what it is to be in need and what it is to have more than enough. I have learned this secret, so that anywhere and at any time, I am content, whether I am full or hungry, whether I have too much or too little". It is believed that Paul wrote these words while in a political prison and not knowing if he would be executed or released, so his words carry a lot of weight in a situation like this. He conveys the fact that our peace does not depend on circumstances but on the state of our mind. We are reminded that if we can't manage to be 'happy' with what we have and where we are right now in this moment, we will not be able to be 'happy' anywhere later.

When in prison, a person has a lot of time to think and meditate. Nelson Mandela was a political prisoner for almost 30 years and said it was the best time of his life because he was able to do the important inner work that he would never have been able to do otherwise. This is such good inspiration for giving ourselves a few short minutes a day to meditate.

According to the Rolling Stones, "We don't always get what we want". So then we are forced into working with what we have and as hard as we try, we sometimes fail in our efforts. We can't always win therefore it would benefit us to learn how to lose without getting bent out of shape and feeling that we are being victimized by the world around us.

Nobody enjoys losing and sometimes we go to great extent in order to avoid it. Just observe the Olympians with all of their hard work and you'll see what I mean. Very few win a Gold Medal and many wind up finishing with nothing but the experience to show for all of their efforts. Are the latter losers? They often feel like they are but in truth, It depends on how they look at it. There is much to be gained from the experience that very few have and the friendships that are formed along the way. Losing is just a different hand that has been dealt and one that challenges them to 'Go with the Flow' and love themselves regardless of the outcome.

For a personal example, in order to deal with the losses that are a natural part of living, I start each day playing 'Spider Solitaire' on my computer. Besides being relaxing, it acts as a meditation for me. I have the chance to observe the unfolding of the game while trying to be unattached to the outcome. It also gives me practice in observing rather than reacting when I lose. Believe me, it is not easy to handle losing in any form but it gets easier when we have practice at it.

One of the greatest benefits of meditation is that it brings balance to the mind.

When we are stuck in one pattern of behavior or another, we are considered to be mentally unbalanced. By observing ourselves through meditation, we become aware of these behaviors and that awareness is the first requirement needed to adjust them.

Diagnostic Manuals provide information about various levels and degrees of mental imbalance. Some are severe and classified as Psychosis. These stem from chemical imbalances in the brain and are treatable with medication and psychotherapy. It is not advisable for a person with Psychosis to meditate because it can bring them to an unmanageable state of overload.

Much more common and less severe are the mental abnormalities of Neurosis. They are something we all have in one degree or another. They are emotional disturbances and often find their roots in our thought processes. When they are most troublesome, they can be treated with cognitive therapy and the learning of coping mechanisms.

Meditation is one of the most effective coping tools that we can use. Through this practice, we are able to see ourselves more objectively and not take everything so personally. It then follows that we become much less reactive to most situations.

Being an Observer instead of a Reactor can solve a multitude of problems.

This statement is based on the fact that we cannot do two things at the same time.

Some say they are able to multitask but that is a physical impossibility. You cannot do two different tasks simultaneously. We cannot have two different thoughts simultaneously.

This idea has many practical applications in regard to dealing with our neurosis by meditating.

For example, let's say that we are dealing with a bout of depression. We can say to ourselves, "I observe that I am having thoughts about being depressed". Once those words are spoken, we have placed ourselves outside of the depression to look at it for the moment and it lowers the intensity of our suffering in the process. Sometimes you can literally feel a shift of awareness in yourself and experience the sense of relief that goes along with it. The trick is to keep observing in order to replace the reacting.

You can test this with most thoughts that bring you discomfort.

Let's say that you are feeling anxious about something that is coming up for you in the near future. You may have a test to take or a presentation to make. You may have a blind date or a job interview. It could be anything that involves facing the unknown. Observe what you are thinking about it and then notice if that makes a difference in how you feel.

Sometimes it helps to write down or journal about what you are observing in order to see it more clearly and disperse the nervous energy that accompanies it. Creating a mandala that pictures what you are fearful about is also very helpful for observing it. But if either of these methods produce more anxiety than expected, they should be followed by writing or creating pictures of things that make you feel safe and calm.

PTS (Post Traumatic Stress) is a little harder to manage with meditation so in this case it should always be used with caution. Those who serve in active combat have the worst experience with PTS but almost everyone can suffer its effects from things like bullying, abuse, accidents, attacks, tragedies, surgery, divorce, or the death of a loved one. We all need extra help and support in these cases but I have found that recordings of guided imagery can be a good supplement to aftercare in these situations.

When we learn how to be good observers by practicing meditation, it can help us in so many practical ways. It has helped me in dealing with shyness. When I plan on going into a social setting alone and fear being too self-conscious I decide to go with the plan of observing everybody else. It is a good substitute for putting the focus on myself and relieves me of a lot of stress.

Observing can be a tremendous help to us in our relationships. For example, if we are at odds with our spouse or partner and having a heated argument about an important issue, we can take a mental step back and observe what is happening rather than being fully engaged in proving that we are right. Again, we can't do two things at the same time. Just being still and observing our partner can help us to see things more objectively and also serves to diffuse the argument almost instantly because there is no one left to argue with. Some things are important enough to fight for but in order to use our precious energy wisely we also need to know how to 'pick our fights'.

Being a good observer can be helpful in other aspects of our relationships as well because it makes us more conscious of ourselves. When we are more aware of our own behavior and realize that we are like all other human beings, we can be more understanding and forgiving of the behavior of others. Did you ever wonder why some people behave badly? Of course it could simply be a matter of human weakness in the moment but, it often goes deeper than that. There is an expression that sheds light on the matter, which is "Hurting people hurt people". If a person strikes out with words or otherwise, it's because they are either chemically imbalanced at the time or someone has previously struck out at them.

There is a common story that shows how this works in an immediate way. A man is yelled at by his boss at work and doesn't feel free to retaliate. He comes home angry and yells at his wife. She doesn't want to get into an argument with him so she unconsciously yells at her child. The child is hurt and kicks the cat. If these characters were conscious of their behavior, the story would have come down in a different way.

Many unresolved hurts are carried over from the past and are often referred to as baggage and this baggage influences our behavior in a big way if we are unaware of it. This lack of awareness has us usually acting just the opposite of the way we are feeling.

We try to hide our hurts and protect ourselves from more of the same. Therefore, if we thought we were inferior as a child, we will come across as superior to others as an adult. We will be defensive and always trying to prove that we are right. If we were depressed and withdrawn we might appear to be outgoing and upbeat to others. This is often the case with comedians. If we were fearful, we will act fearlessly and move with courage to do things that scare us. These are not negative things but are examples of why you shouldn't 'judge a book by its cover' and show compassion toward someone who we think is acting badly.

Everyone wants to be loved and accepted. Giving love and kindness is the best way to get it in return. Many may not have much of it in them to give. It would follow then that their bad behavior is a cry for love. If we can see this in an objective way, we will be less likely to be sucked into confronting the 'Paper Tiger' in front of us and even possibly be able to give it the hug that it needs.

Having a meditation practice helps us in several ways. First, it trains us to be more conscious of our behavior and our actions. Secondly, it enables us to be better aware of our thoughts. The third thing and the hardest one to put into practice is that it helps us to be aware of our words while we are speaking them.

Being self-aware is the best way to improve any of our relationships.

Being a good observer can also help us to alleviate the problem of loneliness.

Being alone is one of the best opportunities we can have to become a good friend to ourselves. But it is among the hardest that many of us will have to learn from because of its painful nature.I have heard people express (even in song) that "I'm so lonely I could die". And having no one to talk to but our self can be dangerous because it doesn't always afford us the best available input. The best solution to this problem would be to put ourselves in social situations regularly, but for one reason or another, it is not always possible.

We are social creatures by nature so we are drawn to live in community and share intimacy with others. However, there are many reasons that account for this not happening. When we are young it's because we haven't yet found the right person that we want to live with. As we get older it might be because of a break up with the person we thought we wanted to live with. When we are even older, it could be because our partner has passed away. Beyond this, there are many that choose to live alone and to lead celibate lives. Those are priests and nuns that take a vow of celibacy. There are young people who are waiting to be married before having sex. There are those who are disabled or paralyzed who have sexual desires but whose bodies are unable to fulfill them.

There are many who live alone by choice or otherwise that have a need for intimacy but not the opportunity to engage in it. There are also those who are married and find their partners are unable to satisfy their needs. Sometimes we turn to food and drugs to dilute the intensity of our feelings but it only hurts us in the long run. We can also try to manually satisfy our own needs but this often leaves us cold. Many use pornography and some go so far as to force themselves on others but these things just keep us trapped in the pursuit of gratification at all cost and to the detriment of others.

We will always be lonely if we think of ourselves as only a body. We are quite a bit more complex than that. We are multi-dimensional beings. Anyone that has done mind altering drugs can attest to that. We have many different levels of subtle energies, always moving around and inside of us. The more we become aware of this, the easier it is to work with them and move thru them.

In far eastern cultures, they have a way of simplifying the complexity of these energies by seeing the body as having seven specific locations from which they move. These start at the base of the spine and end up at the top of the head. They are called Chakras or Energy Centers.

The first one is at the base of the spine and is called our Root Chakra. It is where we feel our sexual energy and is connected to the color red.

The second is in the area of our reproductive organs and where our creativity is centered. It is connected to the color orange.

The third one is located right behind the pit of the stomach in the solar plexus and is where we find the source of our power. It is connected to the color yellow.

The heart is the location of the fourth chakra and is the place that gives us the desire to love and be loved. It is connected to the color green. This is in the middle of the seven centers and is where we find a balance point between the lower and higher energies.

The fifth chakra is found in the throat. It is the center for self-expression, especially in the form of our words. Its color is light blue.

Sixth is where we find what is referred to as our Third Eye. It is located in the middle of the forehead and considered to be the source of intuition. Its color is dark blue.

The seventh location is called the Crown Chakra and is at the very top of our head. It is from here that our Spiritual Energy Flows. Its color is Lavender.

The knowledge of the chakras can be helpful to us because they illustrate a kind of ladder that we can mentally climb in order to move out of our lower urges into a higher state of mind. This movement of focus is called Sublimation and it is accomplished by substituting one thought for another. Reading or viewing something inspirational rather than looking at pornography can help in that endeavor. Offering to help another in place of gratifying our urges, pulls our focus outward and upward. Making music instead of complaining about being deprived can always lift us higher. Spending time in prayer and meditation provides the perfect opportunity to move toward the higher reality within us for our comfort.

The final antidote for loneliness is also found in an awareness of this greater reality. When we are suffering the pangs of loneliness, we are seeing ourselves only as bodies that are separated from the other bodies around us. When we look at ourselves through Spirit Eyes, we are united with everything. We are not separate and never ever can be.

A lot of alternative medicine is aimed at clearing and balancing our bodies through our energy centers. It is believed that our chakras can become congested and cause physical and emotional problems in the specific part of the body that relate to them. Tension can be held in these areas from unresolved physical or emotional trauma. Sometimes we might be holding anger or resentment toward a person or circumstance and in these cases it can help to clear that congestion on our own with forgiveness.

Energy healers are specifically trained with gentle techniques to do this clearing and balancing work. However, there are simple guided meditations that can enable us to do it for ourselves.

The following is a color meditation involving a relaxing mental trip to the ocean that you could safely try.

Before you begin, find a quiet comfortable spot in which to sit or lie down for about five to ten minutes. It is best if you can close your eyes so it would be very helpful to have someone with a soothing voice read it to you. Or you could also make a recording with your own best soothing voice to play back for yourself. This must be read slowly and allowing for the pauses indicated by the dots. If you do make a recording, it can effectively be used later to help you fall asleep at night. You can even record soft music or ocean waves behind your voice to make it better.

Close your eyes and begin to follow your breath as it comes in and out of your body. Give yourself the suggestion that each time you exhale, you become more and more relaxed . . . . The next time you breathe in, go to that spot in the center of yourself where you feel very calm and quiet . . . . Imagine in that spot, that there is a very small bubble and with each breath it becomes larger and larger until it surrounds your body. . . . . The bubble is light and you are light within it. It lifts you off the ground where you are sitting and carries you into the air. . . . . It slowly floats through the sky . . . . . past clouds. . . . . and takes you toward the ocean . . . . There the bubble slowly and gently lowers you to the ground on the beach . . . . You step out of the bubble and breathe in the wonderful sea air. . . . . Then look for a good spot in which to lie down and get into a comfortable position . . . . The water is just gently washing up over your toes . . . . You are alone there – the beach is all yours . . . . You are very comfortable as you lay on the beach . . . . .The sun is shining down on you and warming you with its rays . . . .

The light from the sun gradually becomes a vibrant red color. . . . You are bathed in the light of the sun and its beautiful red hue. . . . . . . .You don't need to open your eyes to know that everything is bathed in this beautiful red light. . . . . . the trees, the sand, the sky and the waves . . . . . .You just lay there and soak in the red light . . . .

The red light slowly turns into orange and you are bathed in the orange light of the sun . . . . and everything around you is orange. . . . . . . You quietly breathe in the orange color around you. . . . .

The orange slowly becomes yellow . . . . . . You are bathed in the beautiful yellow light of the sun. . . . . . Everything around you glows in a golden yellow light and you breathe in the golden air as you lay there on the beach. . . . .

The yellow slowly turns into a rich lovely green and you are bathed in the light of the green sun. . . . . .It turns everything around you into a beautiful emerald green color. . . . .You breath in the green and are nourished by its light . . . .

The green slowly turns to Blue . . . . . It's a gentle blue that makes everything glow in its light . . . . The sky is blue . . . the trees . . . and the sand . . . . and you are bathed in the beautiful blue light of the sun . . . . . You breathe in and absorb its calm and soft light . . . .

The light blue begins to deepen in to a darker blue color and you are surrounded by a beautiful deep blue light . . . . You breath in its richness and beauty . . . .

.The deep blue sky softly turns into a lovely lavender color . . . . . you are bathed in the lavender rays of the sun . . . . . . and everything around you is this gentle lavender color . . . . . . You breathe in the beauty of the lavender around you . . . .

The lavender slowly fades and everything returns to its natural color. . . . . You very slowly get up from the beach and step back into the bubble that is there for you . . . . As you sit in the bubble, it gently lifts off the ground and into the air . . . . It quietly floats thru the sky past the clouds in the direction that it came from . . . . It comes back into the place where you are sitting and gently sets you down there. . . . The bubble gets smaller and smaller and comes back to the place deep within you . . . . When you are ready, slowly open your eyes and being refreshed and alert, return to the space and the time where you are.

Watercolor 8″ x 10″   by Sister Carolyn Wiethorn CSJ 1985

Observe and just Breathe

WHO ARE YOU?

"Oh God, help me to believe the truth about myself, no matter how beautiful it is"
~Macrina Weiderkher – Benedictine Nun

'Who are you' is not a simple question because there are so many different ways that it can be answered. We can base it on our ethnicity or gender. We can identify ourselves by our religion, politics or profession. Some define themselves with their gifts or even disabilities.

The answers also change over time depending on where we are in our stage of development.

If you ask a young child who they are, they will give you their name. When they start school, they will identify themselves as a student in a particular grade. As a teenager who is going through an important phase of understanding their identity, they will often see themselves as part of a certain group like a debate club, a sports team or even a gang. In young adulthood, we often claim our identity as a student of a trade school or university that we attend. And these are all valid answers for the time that they are asked and given.

As adults, we most often tend to identify ourselves with our jobs or the kind of work we do. We are proud of our accomplishments and if we have well-earned letters, we attach them to our name so that we can be easily identified and respected for our particular profession, and rightly so. As we age and retire from the normal work force, there is a whole new search for identity and purpose that occurs.

Along our way, others give us input about who they think we are. If we are impressionable, this has a strong influence on the way we see and identify ourselves. This applies whether it is positive or negative and tends to stick with us all of our lives. What power words can have!

But most often we are given subjective input and if it impacts our lives negatively, it is worth taking a good hard look at in order to question its validity for us.

We are complex beings who can never be defined with one word. No one is just an idiot or a genius, a devil or an angel. We are all capable of being those things, but there is far more to us than a single adjective.

Nobody is just one thing. It doesn't include the entire truth to define ourselves or others by the work we do or by our nicknames or personality traits. Neither does it do us justice to say that we are a success or failure. All this is about how we are perceived in the outside world. If we solely identify with that, it blocks us from seeing our inner, truer reality and from knowing that we are far more than what meets the eye.

Those that are religious or spiritual in their outlook are more aware of this. They will identify themselves in a larger context and being part of a group or Sangha such as a Church or synagogue or temple is an important way to support an awareness of this broader view.

Meditation also brings us to an awareness of the bigger picture of who we are. By repeatedly observing our thoughts, we discover that they change at record breaking speed. These are the very thoughts that go into making the stories that we use to identify our outer selves.

But if these thoughts and stories change so quickly, can they be all that reliable? We come to realize that they are quite unstable and in large part.....illusions.

At the same time, when we meditate and quiet our thoughts, we are afforded the chance to feel the stillness within ourselves where it is calm and peaceful. It is a place beyond all the changing stories, where there are no stories at all. There is nothing beginning and nothing ending. It is just a profound Stillness where we feel safe and complete. Is this where our Soul lives? Is this what we really are? I'm putting my money on that.

The more we understand the totality of what we are, the more empowered we become. The more awareness we have of our Spiritual Nature, the less afraid we are of what can hurt our bodies. We don't even need to fear death because we know that our real identity is in our soul and that can never be harmed.

If we are able to grasp the reality of the Spiritual Nature of ourselves, we will be able to see it in others and come to understand that we are interconnected and all One because of it.

When we look at it in this way, our sameness is recognized and our differences are diminished. We will be able to come to a point that when we look at each other, it is as though we are looking in a mirror and what we see is a reflection of ourselves - with a different face.

It becomes easier for us to love others when we see them as part of our self and in this loving we fulfill our greatest 'reason for being'.

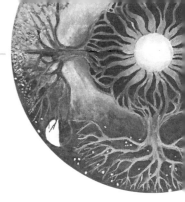

TRANSFORMATION

"Learning how to be still and let life happen, that stillness becomes radiance"
~Morgan Freeman

Wholeness, strength and radiance already exist in all of us. We have been told that the Kingdom of Heaven is within us. So it's not a task of trying to make it happen but more a matter of being still long enough to be able to recognize it. This takes some practice however.

Meditation is often referred to as a mindfulness practice. It is not something we do once and then become magically enlightened. It takes time and repeated action for transformation to occur. When a student of Michelangelo asked him how he could also be a great artist like his teacher, he was told to continually practice with the words: "Every day, Draw Antonio, Draw!"

My father was a professional accordion player and made very beautiful music. Besides entertaining others with his band, he would play and sing love songs to my mother in the evenings before we went to bed. When I was young, I wanted to be just like him and after repeatedly asking, he bought me a small size accordion when I was in the first grade.

He began to teach me how to play but when he pointed out a mistake, I would cry from thinking I was disappointing him. Since we weren't making much progress that way, he found a teacher that I could study with on a weekly basis and did so for the next twelve years until I graduated from high school. During that time, I practiced every day with very few exceptions.

I got to be very accomplished, enough so that I was able to compete in one of the early talent shows on TV when I was only twelve years old. I actually won in the first round of elimination by playing a nifty rendition of "The Hawaiian War Chant". I was prevented from getting too 'puffed up' however because I was beaten in the second round by an older man who played Spoons on his knees.

I didn't practice all those years because I was forced into it. I did it because I really wanted to be a good player like my dad. It was difficult in the beginning as it is with anything that we start new, but it got easier each time I did it. The point is, consistency and practice really do pay off.

Why should we devote ourselves to a practice of meditation? It isn't a quick fix to make us high. It isn't something that we can do once and get it accomplished. It isn't something that brings us Kudos for our efforts. Nobody pays us for our time spent and sometimes we can even come under suspicion for the doing of it. It is a path we choose because there is a goal that we are working toward. It is different for different people. For me it was to manage anxiety and depression. For some it's a way to relax and rejuvenate. For others it is to get to know themselves better and be able to see things more clearly. As it so happens, that in choosing any one of these goals, as we practice, we gain them all.

Choose a practice that feels right for you and be encouraged to begin. You have the support of Mother Nature behind you. Transformation is always happening all by itself. It is a natural part of everything that grows. When we meditate, we are simply co-operating with the unfolding of Life. Of course it isn't all about observing life as it goes by. There are things that are within our power to control and require that we take responsibility for them.

If we take a close look however, we will notice that there are many things that are out of our control and many that are just none of our business. These are the things that present the bulk of our work in meditation. These are the things that invite us to just be in the moment and relax into 'what is'.

Time for another deep breath!

The Butterfly with its metamorphosis speaks beautifully about how the natural process of Transformation occurs. When it is a caterpillar, it is very busy sustaining itself but has some inner knowing that it is something greater than a worm. That knowing is what pulls it toward spinning a cocoon in which to hide and let nature take its course. It may appear to be in a passive state but in that still dark place, it is doing the work that it has been born for. It is yielding to the disintegration of the idea of itself as a caterpillar in order to reform itself into the reality of the butterfly that it is.

In essence this is what we do when we meditate. This yielding is not a negative thing. It is a matter of setting aside a smaller idea of ourselves for a bigger and truer one. In your efforts, keep hope strong and be patient because like the caterpillar, we will eventually morph into the best version of ourselves.

Just don't give up before the miracle happens!

"Passing Through" 24"x 18"   Dot painting by TMDove 2010

"We are all visitors to this time, this place. We are just passing through.
Our purpose here is to Observe, to Learn, to Grow, to Love....and then
We return Home."

~Aboriginal Proverb

Printed in the United States
by Baker & Taylor Publisher Services